Communication Effectiveness Profile

Dr. Jon Warner

HRD Press • Amherst • Massachusetts

Copyright © 2010, Team Publications. All rights reserved.

Published by: HRD Press, Inc.
                22 Amherst Road
                Amherst, MA 01002
                (800) 822-2801 (U.S. and Canada)
                (413) 253-3488
                (413) 253-3490 (Fax)
                http://www.hrdpress.com

In association with Team Publications.

All rights reserved. Any reproduction of this material in any media without written permission of the publisher is a violation of international copyright law.

ISBN: 0-87425-668-2

Cover design by Eileen Klockars
Production services by Anctil Virtual Office

Introduction and Instructions

Most of us take the art of **Communication** for granted. And why shouldn't we? After all, we take part in dozens of conversations each and every day. It ought to be something we're relatively good at! The truth is that most of us are not as good at two-way communication as we think we are.

Our success or failure to communicate effectively will shape and perhaps determine whether or not we achieve our personal and professional goals. It will affect our self-esteem and our sense of well-being, and the contributions we make to our families, our jobs, and our communities. Good or bad communication can even affect our health.

Leonardo da Vinci, Pablo Picasso, Ludwig von Beethoven, John Steinbeck, Maya Angelou, Stephen Spielberg, and other respected writers, musicians, and artists weren't born successful communicators. It took years of study, practice, and commitment to achieve a level of excellence in self-expression. Like art, effective communication is based on several fundamental principles—common sense, really. If we understand these basic skills and then *practice and refine them* so that we are able to put them to use depending on the situations we find ourselves in, we will become quite adept at the art.

The *way* we communicate is tied to how we perceive a situation or an issue, and this "view" is shaped in large part by our values and beliefs. Our upbringing, educational experiences, socio-economic status, religion, and politics—all these things form the basis of our values and beliefs. We need to understand the "spin" our values and beliefs are putting on the conversations and interactions we have with others. Some of it might stand in the way of understanding and productive communication.

This questionnaire has been designed as a self-scoring Communication Effectiveness assessment that will help individuals understand more about their skills in this critical area. Research has shown that there are seven factors that contribute to good (or bad) communication. These are:

- **Empathizing**
- **Receiving the Message**
- **Clarifying**
- **Understanding**
- **"Reading" Nonverbal Clues**
- **Giving and Receiving Feedback**
- **Transmitting Your Message**

These competency areas represent critical skills involved in effective communication. Each area is explained briefly in the paragraph under each respective heading.

Copyright © 2010, Team Publications
Published by HRD Press, Inc. 800-822-2801
22 Amherst Road, Amherst, MA 01002. All rights reserved.
Any reproduction of this material in any media without written permission of the publisher is a violation of international copyright law.

Completing This Booklet

This questionnaire will be easy to complete. Read each introductory paragraph to understand the competency, and select the 1, 2, 3, 4, or 5 rating that best represents your response to each question. Shade in that box and all the boxes "below" it. (Do not shade in part of a box.) For example, if you score the item "I maintain good eye contact and give people my full attention" as a "4" (meaning "very frequently"), shade in *the first four boxes* on the left. If you score it "1" (meaning "almost never"), shade in the first box from the left. You will be creating a bar graph or "histogram" to give you a quick visual reference of your scores.

The scale for each category will always be 1–5, extending from "almost never" or 1 on the left to "almost always" or 5 on the right. Once you have answered all 12 questions in the category, you will be able to draw conclusions about how well you communicate.

As a final step, add up all of your scores and divide them by 12 (the total number of questions). Shade in the aggregate score box the same way you did the others; this time, your score will be precise (3.7, for example). Shade in part of a box here, if you have to.

After you have shaded in the response boxes, look at the Interpretation notes at the bottom of the page. These notes will explain the likely impact of certain scores, and suggest ways to improve any weak areas. The shorter the bar on the histogram, the more you need to improve in that particular aspect of communication. Be sure you read the notes for all seven sections (one competency area on each page).

After you have completed and read the interpretation notes for all seven sections, turn to page 10 and plot your scores on the "spider" diagram. Once you have connected all of the points, you will create your overall Communication profile. Then add up all the aggregate scores from all the sections and divide by 7. Enter your total "Communication Effectiveness" score in the box provided.

Page 10 provides additional suggestions regarding things you can do to improve weak areas.

The Personal Action Plan checklist provided on page 11 will help individuals develop a written plan to address some of the items and issues identified by the assessment. Copy this page and give it to a friend or a family member and ask them to check (after 3 months or so) whether or not you have implemented/are implementing your improvement plan.

This booklet is yours to complete and keep as a reference document. Remember, your overall profile is likely to change over time; what you fill in about yourself today might not apply in three, six, or twelve months. However, if you are honest with yourself, this profile will serve as an accurate picture of your overall ability to communicate effectively, and help you identify where you should concentrate your efforts to improve. You can fill out another assessment in the future to see how far you progressed.

Empathizing

This section on Empathizing examines the extent to which you think about the perspectives and feelings of others when they are communicating with you, and the degree to which you adjust your style to accommodate them. This category asks the question: "How well do you create a climate of warmth and sincerity, where people feel comfortable sharing their thoughts because they know you will listen?"

Please complete this part of the questionnaire as honestly as possible. It can help you improve your ability to communicate effectively. The choice scales are as follows:

1 = almost never; 2 = occasionally; 3 = frequently; 4 = very frequently; 5 = almost always.

Fill in all the boxes up to the score you select so you create a shaded bar.

	Almost Never				Almost Always
	1	2	3	4	5
1. I maintain good eye contact and give people my full attention.					✓
2. I smile warmly at people when they appear to want to talk to me.				✓	
3. I let people finish what they are saying without interrupting.			✓		
4. I think about *why* as well as *what* people are saying.					✓
5. I show genuine interest when people are talking to me, whatever the subject or topic.					✓
6. I use a variety of careful questioning approaches to help understand the other person.		✓			
7. I generally mirror people's facial expressions when I listen to them.		✓			
8. I engage in as much "small talk" as necessary to help people feel comfortable.					✓
9. I like to find out something about the people with whom I talk.			✓		
10. I look at the feelings or emotions behind the words people are using.					✓
11. People who know me would say that I am a sincere and genuine communicator.					✓
12. I encourage people to speak their minds openly and share their concerns.					✓

(Add up all the column scores and divide by 12) **AGGREGATE SCORE**

4 1/12

INTERPRETATION

Scales predominantly in the fours and fives ("very frequently" and "almost always") suggest that you naturally generate a spirit of warmth toward others, and offer lots of help and support in facilitating an easy "flow" of two-way conversation. You usually listen attentively and adapt or adjust your personal style to suit the situation as much as necessary to create the best possible climate.

Scales predominantly in the ones and twos ("almost never" and "occasionally") suggest that you have a more "transactional" communication style, where a discussion or conversation is only a functional exchange of words. You are not likely to consider any circumstantial context or feelings, and you show a tendency to push your own agenda or communication priorities at the expense of the other party.

IMPACT

An individual who scores low in this area will usually keep their communication very direct, putting personal outcomes or needs very much at the forefront. They tend to interrupt frequently and guess what the other person is going to say before he or she says it. Because of this, they often miss important parts of the overall message and create the impression that they have only a limited attention span for deeper or more complex issues.

A high score indicates that the individual is likely to spend as much time as necessary engaging in "small talk" or conversation that helps them understand where the other party is coming from so they can offer supportive and insightful comments that can help to open up the discussion. This means that they will seek to establish the most appropriate communication climate for the circumstances, and offer an empathetic ear.

ACTION FOR LOW SCORERS

Low scorers need to develop an ability to generate more warmth and sincerity in all their conversation, and show genuine care and interest in what other people have to say on a consistent basis. This will involve being more patient, taking more time to engage in "small talk," and trying to appreciate the other person's feelings and emotions just as much as the words that they hear.

Receiving the Message

This section on Receiving the Message looks at how well you listen to and successfully "process" what others are saying (verbal and nonverbal messages) before you respond. This category asks the question: "How attentive or empathetic are you in a listening situation so that you can fully appreciate what the speaker is trying to convey?"

Please complete this part of the questionnaire as honestly as possible. It can help you improve your ability to communicate effectively. The choice scales are as follows:

        1 = almost never; 2 = occasionally; 3 = frequently; 4 = very frequently; 5 = almost always.

Fill in all the boxes up to the score you select so you create a shaded bar.

	Almost Never				Almost Always
	1	2	3	4	5
1. I avoid interrupting while the other person is speaking.		✓			
2. I make sure that I'm in the right frame of mind for all important discussions.					✓
3. I try to find quiet environments in which to talk and listen to people.					✓
4. My body language is conducive to attentive listening.				✓	
5. I listen enthusiastically and positively.				✓	
6. I avoid trivializing the ideas or views expressed by people I am talking with.		✓			
7. I look people in the eye and regularly nod in order to demonstrate that I have understood them.					✓
8. I focus my attention on the speaker and concentrate on what is being said.				✓	
9. I try not to let my mind wander when someone is talking to me.		✓			
10. I am calm and patient in conversation and discussion.				✓	
11. I take information in on several different "channels" where necessary.					✓
12. People who know me well would say that I am a good listener.				✓	

(Add up all the column scores and divide by 12) **AGGREGATE SCORE**: 3¾

INTERPRETATION

Scales predominantly in the fours and fives ("very frequently" and "almost always") suggest that you are an attentive listener and appreciate the "tenor" of most communications, in whatever form they are conveyed. You are genuinely interested and you try to concentrate on what people are saying, maintaining a calm and patient demeanor so people can get their message across without interruption.

Scales predominantly in the ones and twos ("almost never" and "occasionally") suggest that you do not always fully appreciate what people communicate, and thus you miss important components of the overall message. You are also prone to being easily distracted, and tend to jump into conversations before the other person has finished speaking.

IMPACT

An individual who scores low in this area is likely to find communication frustrating or even confusing. This is sometimes the speaker's fault, but more likely it is one result of poor listening habits—the listener hasn't focused or taken enough time to "hear" the complete message, and the mind has been allowed to wander to other things and other priorities or tasks.

A high score suggests that the individual is an appreciative and attentive listener who freely gives all their attention to the speaker in order to hear and appreciate the complete message. A person who scores high in this area makes an especially valuable contribution when important or complex information needs to be communicated for insight or comment.

ACTION FOR LOW SCORERS

Low scorers need to speak less and listen more. To do this, they need to find more-conducive listening environments, avoid interrupting, and keep their minds from wandering. Most of all, they need to try to quietly hear the whole message being communicated, without jumping in too soon.

Clarifying

This section on Clarifying looks at the extent to which you use careful and incisive questioning techniques to successfully "translate" the words and actions of the other party in order to understand their meaning. This category asks the question: "How well do you gently question and probe the other person in a conversation or discussion, in order to ensure that you accurately interpret their message?"

Please complete this part of the questionnaire as honestly as possible. It can help you improve your ability to communicate effectively. The choice scales are as follows:

1 = almost never; 2 = occasionally; 3 = frequently; 4 = very frequently; 5 = almost always.

Fill in all the boxes up to the score you select so you create a shaded bar.

	Almost Never				Almost Always
	1	2	3	4	5
1. I avoid making the other person feel as if he or she is being interrogated.					✓
2. I look for the underlying message behind people's words.				✓	
3. I try to use "word pictures" when clarifying what the speaker seems to be saying.		✓			
4. I gently get the speaker to provide "missing" information as a conversation flows.					✓
5. I regularly paraphrase to test my understanding of what is being said.				✓	
6. I carefully probe when I do not fully understand something.			✓		
7. I use open questions to get people to explain their ideas.				✓	
8. I demonstrate that I can be helpful and genuine in conversations.					✓
9. People who know me would say that I ask incisive questions in conversations.				✓	
10. I summarize what I think I've heard to make sure that I have understood clearly.					✓
11. I am comfortable speaking up when I am confused or unsure.					✓
12. I offer my interpretation of what is being said in order to verify my understanding of what is being communicated.					✓

56

(Add up all the column scores and divide by 12) **AGGREGATE SCORE**

4 ⅔

INTERPRETATION

Scales predominantly in the fours and fives ("very frequently" and "almost always") suggest that you are skilled at using a variety of conversational techniques in order to check information without making the other party uncomfortable, or feel that they are being interrogated. You generally adopt a gentle and careful questioning approach whenever you feel unsure and are not clear about the message being transmitted.

Scales predominantly in the ones and twos ("almost never" and "occasionally") suggest that you rarely use questions to increase your understanding, or your questions are somewhat vague or give the impression that you have not been listening or are not interested in all they have to say.

IMPACT

An individual with a low score generally engages in highly "transactional" discussions and conversations; questions of clarification are asked only rarely. These individuals are unlikely to summarize or paraphrase the sender's message, thus creating the impression that their mind is elsewhere. They will usually ask questions only when they want more information on subjects that are of interest to them.

A high score suggests that the individual is likely to create a climate in which the speaker sees that the listener is concentrating and trying to completely understand the communication. This is achieved by using questions to demonstrate openness and demonstrating a genuine desire to understand, rather than showing off superior knowledge or asking a question for the sake of saying something.

ACTION FOR LOW SCORERS

Low scorers need to practice asking genuine and sincere questions when their understanding in a discussion is less than it should be. They should also practice asking different kinds of questions and offer simple summaries of key points at appropriate conversational intervals.

Understanding

This section on Understanding looks at the extent to which you make sense of what you see and hear in order to engage fully in a conversation and respond intelligently, according to the circumstances. This category asks the question: "How well do you reflect and process information while someone is speaking, in order to understand the key aspects of what is being communicated and how you might respond?"

Please complete this part of the questionnaire as honestly as possible. It can help you improve your ability to communicate effectively. The choice scales are as follows:

1 = almost never; 2 = occasionally; 3 = frequently; 4 = very frequently; 5 = almost always.

Fill in all the boxes up to the score you select so you create a shaded bar.

	Almost Never				Almost Always
	1	2	3	4	5
1. I avoid assuming that the other person's perspective is the same as mine.				✓	
2. I give people time, attention, and encouragement so they can get their message across.					✓
3. I respect other people's feelings when I offer my comments.			✓		
4. I piece together all the different parts of what people say and do to make sense of it.				✓	
5. I ask the other person to re-phrase their message when I am confused.			✓		
6. I suspend judgment about what is being said for as long as necessary.				✓	
7. I correctly identify the level of someone's feelings and emotions in a conversation.				✓	
8. I am good at reading "between the lines" wherever necessary.				✓	
9. I connect what people say to me with what I already know in order to achieve a better understanding.				✓	
10. I carefully follow the flow of a conversation so I can respond appropriately.		✓		✗	
11. I seek to put what I hear into a reasonable context, based on my experience.				✓	
12. I expect conversation and discussion to improve my knowledge and understanding.					✓

(Add up all the column scores and divide by 12) **AGGREGATE SCORE**

30
12
6
2
50

4 ⅛

INTERPRETATION

Scales predominantly in the fours and fives ("very frequently" and "almost always") suggest that you carefully sift and sort what you see and hear when individuals are talking, and work hard to understand the entire message and respond in a way that amply demonstrates your understanding.

Scales predominantly in the ones and twos ("almost never" and "occasionally") suggest that you tend to be lost in longer or more-complex conversations, and fail to spot the more subtle or underlying messages that are communicated. You do not usually take the opportunity to reduce or eliminate your confusion by asking questions, paraphrasing, or summarizing.

IMPACT

A low scorer does not always follow another person's line of discussion or argument and doesn't find it easy to predict where the conversation is headed. As a result, they don't participate as actively in a conversation as they might and their responses are not as helpful and intelligent as they could be.

A high scorer uses empathetic listening techniques and recognizes that they should not make judgments regarding how other people think or send their messages. They will progressively assemble the information that is communicated, and look beyond the words to feelings, emotions, and other contextual factors.

ACTION FOR LOW SCORERS

Low scorers should take all the verbal and non-verbal clues and figure out what is really being said, and why. They also should concentrate more on the overall "flow" or logical development of each conversation, and ask questions and paraphrase to be sure they are not misunderstanding the message.

"Reading" Nonverbal Clues

This section on "Reading Nonverbal Clues" looks at the extent to which you pick up on body language and tone of voice in order to understand the complete communication message. It asks the question: "How well do you assess the other person's feelings and meaning by looking beyond the spoken words that you hear?"

Please complete this part of the questionnaire as honestly as possible. It can help you improve your ability to communicate effectively. The choice scales are as follows:

1 = almost never; 2 = occasionally; 3 = frequently; 4 = very frequently; 5 = almost always.

Fill in all the boxes up to the score you select so you create a shaded bar.

	Almost Never				Almost Always
	1	2	3	4	5
1. I quickly sense when a person's feelings do not match his or her words.			✓		
2. I can tell when the other party is distracted or their mind is somewhere else.					✓
3. I can tell when the climate for open communication is not quite right.				✓	
4. I am good at "reading" other people.				✓	
5. I watch people's facial expressions and hand movements very carefully.				✓	
6. I adjust my communication style if I feel that I am losing the other person's attention.					✓
7. I am good at sensing a negative atmosphere when I walk into a room.			✓		
8. Inconsistencies between words and body language are easy for me to identify.				✓	
9. I quickly notice changes in tone or pitch.			✓		
10. I try to pick up on an individual's underlying feelings.				✓	
11. I pick up on and understand non-verbal clues and signals.				✓	
12. I can tell when someone is confused about what I'm saying by observing his or her body language.					✓

(Add up all the column scores and divide by 12) **AGGREGATE SCORE** — 4

INTERPRETATION

Scales predominantly in the fours and fives ("very frequently" and "almost always") suggest that you are tuned in to the non-verbal clues or signals that are deliberately or accidentally offered by other people in different kinds of communication. You are usually alert to the signals and are able to interpret them successfully.

Scales predominantly in the ones and twos ("almost never" and "occasionally") suggest that you generally miss or misinterpret non-verbal clues given by others because you don't appreciate what they mean. Because of this, you are not likely to be good at reading other people, sensing the climate for communication, or spotting general discrepancies between verbal and non-verbal messages.

IMPACT

A low scorer tends to be almost completely reliant on the words that people use in communication (words are only about 10% of the entire meaning) and oblivious to clues from facial expressions, movements of the hands or feet, changes in inflection and tone, and other clues that help paint a complete picture of what people are saying and feeling.

A high scorer focuses as much on non-verbal communication as they do on the words being spoken, and constantly looks for reinforcement of underlying feelings or inconsistency. They tend to almost intuitively "read" people and situations, even where words are few or non-existent.

ACTION FOR LOW SCORERS

Low scorers need to concentrate much more on observing the other person and listening carefully for changes in voice tone or emotional emphasis. This takes considerable practice, as well as commitment and patience, to learn how to do it and then to correctly interpret what is observed.

Giving and Receiving Feedback

This section on Feedback looks at the extent to which you are able to successfully offer constructive feedback *to* others and accept direct feedback *from* others. It asks the question: "How open are you to offering candid feedback to others in a constructive or helpful way, and how capable are you in accepting coaching or guiding communication from others?"

Please complete this part of the questionnaire as honestly as possible. It can help you improve your ability to communicate effectively. The choice scales are as follows:

1 = almost never; 2 = occasionally; 3 = frequently; 4 = very frequently; 5 = almost always.

Fill in all the boxes up to the score you select so you create a shaded bar.

	Almost Never				Almost Always
	1	2	3	4	5
1. I try to make sure that the "air time" in a conversation is equally shared.		✓			
2. I find it easy to get the other person's attention when speaking with them.					✓
3. I provide and welcome feedback because I want to become a more effective communicator.			✓		
4. I am appreciated for my direct and clear communication style.			✓		
5. I openly demonstrate that I appreciate getting feedback from other people.			✓		
6. I avoid engaging in emotional or negative feedback discussions.		✓			
7. I am not concerned about someone's motives for providing feedback.	✓				
8. I focus my attention on the key lesson to be given or taken from the feedback.				✓	
9. I try not to insult or demean the other party when offering critical comments.				✓	
10. I focus on the facts in giving and receiving feedback.				✓	
11. I consider every constructive criticism as an opportunity to improve.				✓	
12. I am sensitive to my needs and the needs of others when communicating.				✓	

(Add up all the column scores and divide by 12) **AGGREGATE SCORE**

3 2/3

INTERPRETATION

Scales predominantly in the fours and fives ("very frequently" and "almost always") suggest that you are a frequent giver and receiver of feedback, and you see it as a positive way to improve communication and knowledge (for yourself and others). You are likely adept at giving feedback to others and in inviting others to give feedback to you (and acting on the valuable advice you receive).

Scales predominantly in the ones and twos ("almost never" and "occasionally") suggest that you are not a frequent giver and receiver of feedback of any sort, and might even go out of your way to avoid making constructive comments to others or letting them offer comments (positive or negative) to you. You might even adopt a silent approach or become evasive when asked to offer or take feedback.

IMPACT

A low scorer is likely to adopt a "closed" communication style in which they offer little or no constructive feedback to others and, in turn, do not expect others to offer feedback to them. Conversations will tend to be somewhat "mechanical" and exchange-oriented, with neither party gaining the benefit of useful guiding or coaching communication.

An individual whose scores here are high is likely to quickly establish as much conversational rapport as possible with the other person. This is usually done by suggesting that they are open to receiving and giving constructive feedback as a means of building strong relationships, as well as by having deeper or more genuinely worthwhile discussions with people.

ACTION FOR LOW SCORERS

Low scorers need to accept two-way feedback as a primary means of improving the quality of communication. This means becoming less "thin-skinned" about feedback and more open to giving people honest but helpful feedback when it is appropriate.

Transmitting Your Message

This section on Transmitting Your Message looks at the extent to which you use a range of communication methods and means to get your message across to others successfully. It asks the question: "How well do you ensure that the transmission of information that is important to you is communicated in language that is clear, concise, and consistent?"

Please complete this part of the questionnaire as honestly as possible. It can help you improve your ability to communicate effectively. The choice scales are as follows:

1 = almost never; 2 = occasionally; 3 = frequently; 4 = very frequently; 5 = almost always.

Fill in all the boxes up to the score you select so you create a shaded bar.

	Almost Never				Almost Always
	1	2	3	4	5
1. I communicate feelings as well as ideas and facts.					✓
2. I use multiple channels to get messages across to people.					✓
3. I make sure my deeds match my words.				✓	
4. I find that I can lift team spirit and morale through effective communication.					✓
5. I am able to get complicated ideas across clearly.					✓
6. I deliver my communication at a pace and in a way that is comfortable for others.			✓		
7. I say things in a variety of slightly different ways in order to reinforce what I mean.					✓
8. I am very aware of the other person's needs.				✓	
9. I change and vary my communication style, according to the situation.					✓
10. I find the "right" words for the circumstances.		✓			
11. I select the most appropriate method to transmit my messages.				✓	
12. I avoid using jargon, "gobbledegook," and inappropriate language.				✓	

(Add up all the column scores and divide by 12) **AGGREGATE SCORE**

INTERPRETATION

Scales predominantly in the fours and fives ("very frequently" and "almost always") suggest that you think carefully about the way you transmit your message and the communication style that you adopt in order to communicate effectively. To do this, you try hard to always be clear, concise, and consistent in what you say and do.

Scales predominantly in the ones and twos ("almost never" and "occasionally") suggest that you are prone to forget the needs of different audiences to which you communicate. You also do not always select the most appropriate communication channels (you use mainly one single communication or delivery style, regardless of the situation).

IMPACT

For a low scorer, communication is a challenge—something to get over-and-done-with as quickly as possible. Transmitting your message is regarded as a chore that often yields mixed results in terms of other people listening or understanding and acting appropriately on what they have heard.

A high scorer is usually acutely aware of the power to communicate and influence people successfully through good preparation, understanding of the audience's needs, and use of a variety of ways to communicate to ensure that every individual is given the best opportunity to appreciate the message.

ACTION FOR LOW SCORERS

Low scorers need to think more about different individual and group preferences in terms of receiving information, and should think about the impact that different channels and styles can make on the ultimate understanding of a message (and, therefore, the success of the entire communication effort).

General Interpretation

The scores from each of the seven competency areas on the previous pages will combine to create a small histogram when the blocks are shaded in, with the composite score at the bottom of each section being the average of the twelve scores (total scores in the category divided by 12). Averages of 4 or more in each category are good, scores of 2 to 4 should bear further thought and reflection, and scores of less than 2 are in need of attention and deserve immediate focus. In an overall sense, each section is a self-contained mini-questionnaire in its own right. Your average scores for all seven competency areas can be plotted alongside one another on the chart below:

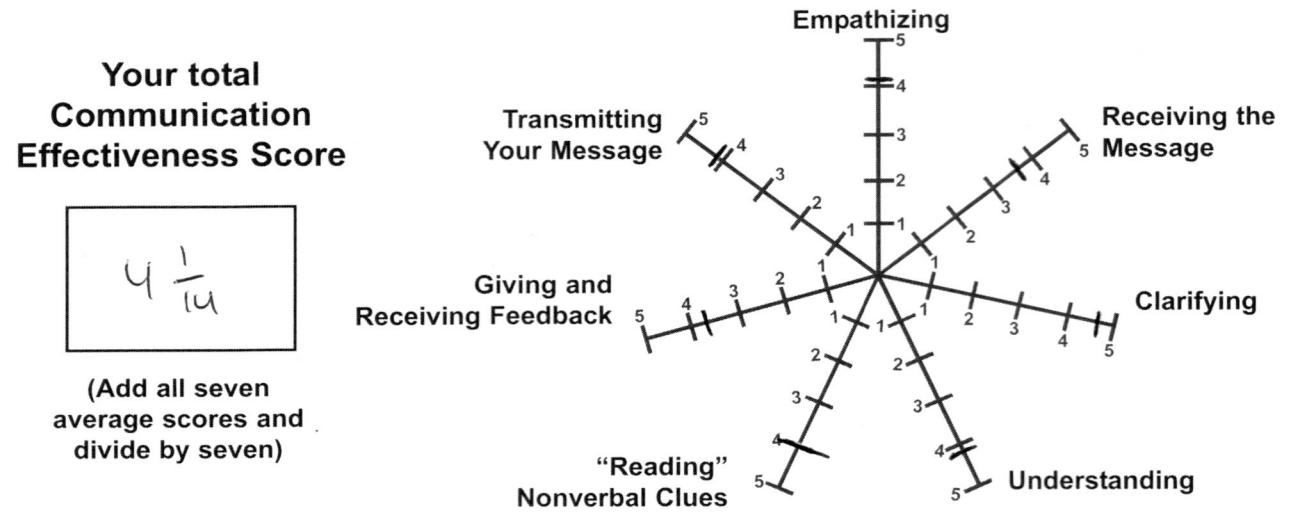

Your total Communication Effectiveness Score

$4\frac{1}{14}$

(Add all seven average scores and divide by seven)

Plot your average score in each competency area on each corresponding axis and connect the crosses to create a quick diagrammatic view of your overall Communication Profile. The further your scores are from the center, the better. Efforts to start improving your communication skills can be concentrated where scores are lowest (generally less than 3). Although there is no prescriptive strategy that can be recommended for everyone (you must develop your own personal plan), general actions to be taken in each category are as follows:

Empathizing	Try to smile at people more often, and be as friendly and sincere as you can when they are talking to you. Make a strong effort to put yourself in the other person's position and imagine what they might be feeling or where they might be coming from.
Receiving the Message	Nod or show in other ways that you have understood at regular points in any conversation. Maintain as much direct eye contact as you can and show genuine and focused interest in the communication. Generally avoid showing any distraction—physical or mental.
Clarifying	Rehearse asking questions in a variety of different ways to get people to say more or to elaborate fully on what they mean. This can involve using more paraphrasing, using examples or analogies, or asking the other person directly to explain what they are saying in a different way.
Understanding	Avoid judging another person's message or intentions too quickly: concentrate on the entire communication over as long a time as is necessary. Also look for key themes or core points in conversations, and use questions to confirm your understanding before responding.
"Reading" Nonverbal Clues	Quietly watch for the more subtle signals given by the communicator in terms of their physical actions or the tone of their voice. To do this, you must be silent for much longer than you are used to as you progressively learn what the different nonverbal signals mean. The words constitute about 10% of the message!
Giving and Receiving Feedback	Think of giving and receiving regular constructive feedback as one of the primary ways that we learn and improve. Make notes on what you hear and offer feedback to others. Frequently invite other people to offer open feedback to you.
Transmitting Your message	Recognize that your actions are likely to speak the loudest when you are communicating to others. You therefore should do things to support your verbal messages to help people to understand where you are coming from. Also, practice varying your personal communication approach to suit all kinds of different situations.

Personal Action Plan

My overall score is 4 1/14   **Date of Action Plan:** 02/10/2020

The areas most in need of attention (in priority order) and their aggregate scores are:

SCORE   COMPETENCY

1. 3 3/4   Recieving the message
2. 3 3/4   Giving & receiving feedback
3. 4   "Reading" Nonverbal clues

My specific plans for becoming more effective in Competency 1 are:

IMMEDIATELY (✔)   By when

- Step 1: Using effective listening skills on a constant basis.
- Step 2: Looking at non verbal clues to avoid interupting.
- Step 3: Think about what they are saying as oppose to what you think they are saying.

My specific plans for becoming more effective in Competency 2 are:

- Step 1: Giving the other person more air time.
- Step 2: Avoiding emotional or negative feedback
- Step 3: Not looking for mistakes from feedback at buying it positively.

My specific plans for becoming more effective in Competency 3 are:

- Step 1: Noticing changes in tone or pitch
- Step 2: Correctly interpret what is observed
- Step 3: Taking time to notice the atmosphere in the room.

In overall terms, I will stop doing or reduce my involvement in:

1.
2.
3.

Signature _____   Date _____

Action Notes

Now that you have plotted your scores and read the associated descriptions for each competency, use the space below to make a number of action notes for yourself. Ideally, you should focus on areas where the scores are low (weak areas).

ABOUT THE AUTHOR

Jon Warner is a professional manager with over 20 years' experience working with multinational companies in the United Kingdom, Europe, the United States, and Australia. He has been the senior staff member in human resources departments, and has held several professional leadership positions with responsibility for large groups of employees. Jon has in recent years been involved in wide-ranging organizational consultancy work and the pursuit of best-practices leadership for such major organizations as Mobil Oil, Quantas, United Energy, Dow Corning, Coca Cola, Barclays Bank, National Bank, Honda, BTR, Gas and Fuel, Air Products and Chemicals, and Caltex.

Jon is managing director of Team Publications PTY Limited, an international training and publishing company committed to bringing practical and fun-to-use learning material to the worldwide training market, such as the One Page Coach® storyboard-based integrated training packages. He holds a master's degree in Business Administration and a Ph.D. in organizational change and learning, and lives and works on Australia's Gold Coast.

REFERENCES

Bendeich, Jan. 1994. *Workplace Communications.* Woodlands Communications.

Burke, Peter. 1993. *The Art of Conversation.* New York: Cornell University Press.

Condrill, Jo and Bennie Bough. 1998. *101 Ways to Improve Your Communication Skills Instantly.* Goalminds.

Hybels, Sandra and Richard Weaver. 1997. *Communicating Effectively.* McGraw Hill (5th edition).

Misteil, Sean. 1997. *The Communicator's PocketBook.* Management PocketBooks.

Westra, Mathew. 1996. *Active Communication.* Brooks/Cole Publishing.